DISCOVER!

ANIMALS THAT SLITHER AND SLIDE

Slippery NEWTS

BY THERESA EMMINIZER

Please visit our website, www.enslow.com. For a free color catalog of all our high-quality books, call toll free 1-800-398-2504 or fax 1-877-980-4454.

Cataloging-in-Publication Data

Names: Emminizer, Theresa.
Title: Slippery newts / Theresa Emminizer.
Description: New York : Enslow Publishing, 2024. | Series: Animals that slither and slide | Includes glossary and index.
Identifiers: ISBN 9781978537378 (pbk.) | ISBN 9781978537385 (library bound) | ISBN 9781978537392 (ebook)
Subjects: LCSH: Newts–Juvenile literature.
Classification: LCC QL668.C28 E67 2024 | DDC 597.8'5–dc23

Published in 2024 by
Enslow Publishing
2544 Clinton Street
Buffalo, NY 14224

Copyright © 2024 Enslow Publishing

Designer: Leslie Taylor
Editor: Theresa Emminizer

Photo credits: Cover (newt) Jason Mintzer/Shutterstock.com, (slime background) AMarc/Shutterstock.com, (brush stroke) Sonic_S/Shutterstock.com, (slime frame) klyaksun/Shutterstock.com; Series Art (slime blob) Lemberg Vector studio/Shutterstock.com; p. 5 StevenW Wild Media/Shutterstock.com; pp. 7, 15 W. de Vries/Shutterstock.com; p.9 HWall/Shutterstock.com; p.11 Michael LaMonica/Shutterstock.com; p.13 Kazakova Maryian/Shutterstock.com; p.17 Liz Weber/Shutterstock.com; p.19 Milan Zygmunt/Shutterstock.com; p.21 MargieV/Shutterstock.com.

All rights reserved. No part of this book may be reproduced in any form without permission in writing from the publisher, except by a reviewer.

Some of the images in this book illustrate individuals who are models. The depictions do not imply actual situations or events.

Printed in the United States of America

CPSIA compliance information: Batch #CW24ENS: For further information contact Enslow Publishing, at 1-800-398-2504.

CONTENTS

Meet the Newt! 4

First, the Egg 6

Larvae 8

Juvenile 10

Adult 12

All Sorts of Newts! 14

Awesome Adaptations 16

Slippery, Slimy, and Special! 20

Words to Know 22

For More Information 23

Index 24

Boldface words appear in
Words to Know.

MEET THE NEWT!

Newts are small, slippery animals with long, smooth bodies, short legs, and round, paddle-like tails. They often live near fresh water. That's because newts are **amphibians**. They spend part of their life in water and part on land!

Newts' webbed feet and paddle-like tails help them move through the water, where they spend much of their time.

5

FIRST, THE EGG

Female newts lay eggs. Although they can lay hundreds of eggs, the eggs are laid individually, or one at a time! Each egg is placed on an underwater plant. It's covered in jelly to keep it safe.

LARVAE

Newt babies are called larvae. The larvae are fully aquatic, meaning they live underwater. Newt larvae eat snails and tiny water animals such as water fleas. They use **gills** to breathe. As the newts grow out of the larvae stage, their gills **disappear.**

A newt's life has three stages, or parts: larva, **juvenile**, and adult.

9

JUVENILE

Juvenile newts are also called efts. During this stage, newts are terrestrial, which means they live on land. While the aquatic stage of the newt's life usually only lasts a few months, the terrestrial stage is usually a few years long.

Juvenile newts like to spend their time in leaf piles looking for food.

ADULT

Newts reach the adult stage when they are ready to have babies of their own. Male newts wiggle and move their tail to **attract** a mate, or partner for making babies. Adult newts go back to the water to lay their eggs.

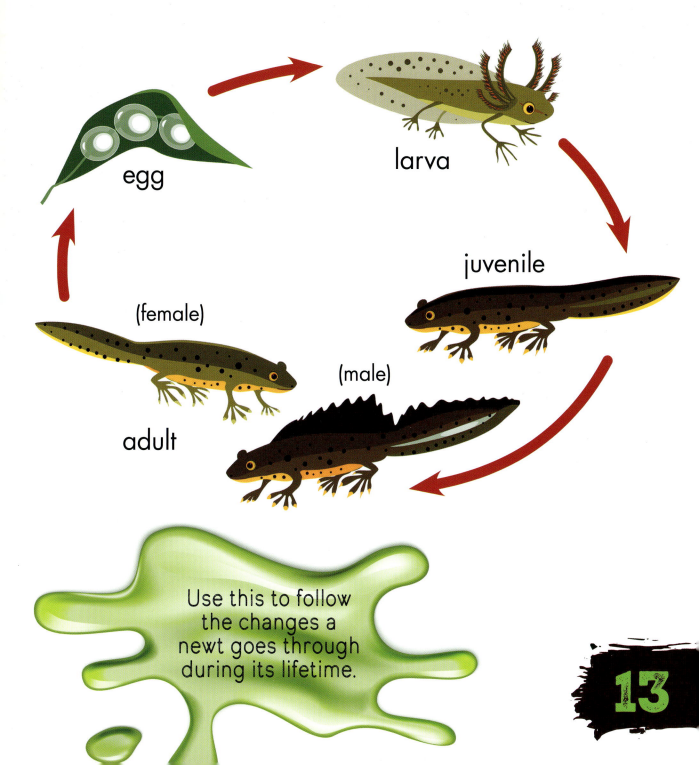

ALL SORTS OF NEWTS!

There are many different species, or kinds, of newts. Some are smaller and others are larger. The biggest newt species is the great crested newt. These animals live in Europe. They can grow to 7 inches (18 cm) long and live up to about 16 years.

AWESOME ADAPTATIONS

Newts have special adaptations, or changes that help them **survive**. For example, they can regenerate, or regrow, parts of their bodies! Newts can regenerate lost limbs (arms and legs), eyes, hearts, and more.

Animals such as foxes and snakes may try to eat newts. Luckily, newts have another special adaptation to keep them safe! Some newts secrete, or let out, **toxins** from their skin. The emperor newt is a very toxic newt species.

SLIPPERY, SLIMY, AND SPECIAL!

Newts are certainly special **creatures**. If you're ever lucky enough to see a newt in nature, it's best not to touch it. Instead, look with wonder at this little animal that has adapted in many special ways to living in its natural settings.

Some people keep newts as pets!

WORDS TO KNOW

amphibian: An animal that spends time on land but must have babies and grow into an adult in water.

attract: Draw in.

creature: An animal or living thing.

disappear: To go away or cease to be.

gill: The body part that water animals such as fish use to breathe in water.

juvenile: Young adult.

survive: To live.

toxin: A kind of poison. Toxic means poisonous or harmful.

FOR MORE INFORMATION

BOOKS

Hughes, Sloane. *Amphibian Adaptations*. New York, NY: Rosen Publishing, 2023.

Morlock, Rachael. *Chinese Salamander: The Largest Amphibian.* New York, NY: PowerKids Press, 2020.

WEBSITES

National Geographic
www.nationalgeographic.com/animals/amphibians/facts/great-crested-newt
Find out more about the great crested newt.

Wonderopolis
www.wonderopolis.org/wonder/what-is-a-newt
Learn more about newts!

Publisher's note to educators and parents: Our editors have carefully reviewed these websites to ensure that they are suitable for students. Many websites change frequently, however, and we cannot guarantee that a site's future contents will continue to meet our high standards of quality and educational value. Be advised that students should be closely supervised whenever they access the internet.

INDEX

babies, 8, 12
body, 4, 16
eft, 10
eggs, 6, 7, 12
emperor newt, 18, 19
food, 8, 11
gills, 8
great crested newt, 14, 15

juvenile, 9, 10, 11, 17
larvae, 8, 9
mate, 12
regeneration, 16
tail, 4, 5
toxins, 18